BILL DAMASCHKE   DORI BERINSTEIN   JACK LANE

JAMES & CATHERINE BERGES   NELDA SUE YAW   NATASHA DAVISON   JOE GRANDY   KIMBERLEE GARRIS   LISA MORRIS   TERRY SCHNUCK
JANE DUBIN   ROSALIND PRODUCTIONS INC.   FAHS PRODUCTIONS   SETH A. GOLDSTEIN   MIKE KRIAK   DON & NANCY ROSS
PAMELA HURST-DELLA PIETRA & STEPHEN DELLA PIETRA   CLIFF HOPKINS   MASIE PRODUCTIONS   VIVEK SHAH   THREE BELLES & A BOB
ARMENT-TACKEL   ARMSTRONG-MANOCHERIAN   FAKLER-SILVER   FOX THEATRICALS-MOSBACHER-LONOW   PALITZ-STERN-SMEDES
NANCY & KEN KRANZBERG/DAVID LYONS   LARRY & ELIZABETH LENKE/ELIZABETH L. GREEN   IRIS SMITH/INSTONE PRODUCTIONS
KUHLMAN-KETNER/WALLACE-ATxRANDOMPRODUCTIONS   THE JOHN GORE ORGANIZATION   and THE SHUBERT ORGANIZATION
in association with INDEPENDENT PRESENTERS NETWORK   MARGOT ASTRACHAN   DARREN P. DEVERNA & JEREMIAH J. HARRIS   REAGAN SILBER

present

Book By	Music By	Lyrics By
BOB MARTIN & CHAD BEGUELIN	**MATTHEW SKLAR**	**CHAD BEGUELIN**

Based on an original concept by JACK VIERTEL

BROOKS ASHMANSKAS   BETH LEAVEL   CHRISTOPHER SIEBER
CAITLIN KINNUNEN   ISABELLE McCALLA   MICHAEL POTTS   ANGIE SCHWORER
COURTENAY COLLINS   JOSH LAMON

MARY ANTONINI   COURTNEY BALAN   GABI CAMPO   JERUSHA CAVAZOS   SHELBY FINNIE
JOSH FRANKLIN   SHELDON HENRY   FERNELL HOGAN   JOOMIN HWANG   DAVID JOSEFSBERG
BECCA LEE   WAYNE "JUICE" MACKINS   KATE MARILLEY   VASTHY MOMPOINT   ANTHONY NORMAN
DREW REDINGTON   JACK SIPPEL   TEDDY TOYE   KALYN WEST   BRITTANY ZEINSTRA

Scenic Design	Costume Design	Lighting Design	Sound Design
SCOTT PASK	ANN ROTH MATTHEW PACHTMAN	NATASHA KATZ	BRIAN RONAN

Hair Design	Makeup Design	Casting	Associate Director	Associate Choreographer
JOSH MARQUETTE	MILAGROS MEDINA-CERDEIRA	TELSEY + COMPANY BETHANY KNOX, CSA	CASEY HUSHION	JOHN MACINNIS

Music Director	Additional Orchestrations	Music Arrangements	Vocal Arrangements	Music Coordinator
MEG ZERVOULIS	JOHN CLANCY	GLEN KELLY	MATTHEW SKLAR & MARY-MITCHELL CAMPBELL	HOWARD JOINES

Marketing Direction	Advertising	Digital Marketing	Press Representation
ON THE RIALTO	AKA	SITUATION INTERACTIVE	POLK & CO.

Production Management	Production Stage Manager	Company Manager	General Management
JUNIPER STREET PRODUCTIONS	GLYNN DAVID TURNER	MARC BORSAK	FORESIGHT THEATRICAL AARON LUSTBADER LANE MARSH

Music Supervisor
MARY-MITCHELL CAMPBELL

Orchestrations
LARRY HOCHMAN

Directed and Choreographed by
CASEY NICHOLAW

World Premiere Produced by Alliance Theatre, Atlanta, GA
Susan V. Booth, Artistic Director   Mike Schleifer, Managing Director

The Producers wish to express their appreciation to TDF for its support of this production.

D1602067

ISBN: 978-1-5400-4607-9

Visit Hal Leonard Online at
www.halleonard.com

Contact us:
Hal Leonard
7777 West Bluemound Road
Milwaukee, WI 53213
Email: info@halleonard.com

In Europe, contact:
Hal Leonard Europe Limited
42 Wigmore Street
Marylebone, London, W1U 2RN
Email: info@halleonardeurope.com

In Australia, contact:
Hal Leonard Australia Pty. Ltd.
4 Lentara Court
Cheltenham, Victoria, 3192 Australia
Email: info@halleonard.com.au

CHANGING LIVES

Lyrics by CHAD BEGUELIN
Music by MATTHEW SKLAR

BARRY: *Let's talk process.*

BARRY: When I'm in char-ac-ter I go in-sane.__ I stag-ger, I stam-mer, I sob. I make the au-di-enc-es feel my pain__ and if they don't leave de-pressed,_ then I've not done my job.__

DEE DEE: Each time I find__ a role like

JUST BREATHE

Lyrics by CHAD BEGUELIN
Music by MATTHEW SKLAR

IT'S NOT ABOUT ME

Lyrics by CHAD BEGUELIN
Music by MATTHEW SKLAR

Bright 4 (Fanfare!)

Recitative, a la Eva Peron

DEE DEE:
I want to tell the peo-ple of what-ev-er this town's called I know what's go-ing on here and frank-ly I'm ap-palled. I read three quar-ters of a news sto-ry and knew I had to come! Un-less I'm do-ing *The Mir-a-cle Work-er,*

a la Rachmaninoff

21

DANCE WITH YOU

Lyrics by CHAD BEGUELIN
Music by MATTHEW SKLAR

Gently and conversational, in 2

Freely

EMMA:

I don't want to start a ri - ot. I don't want to blaze a trail. I don't want to be a sym - bol or cau - tion - ar - y tale. I don't want to be a scape - goat for peo - ple to op - pose.

THE ACCEPTANCE SONG

Lyrics by CHAD BEGUELIN
Music by MATTHEW SKLAR

YOU HAPPENED

Lyrics by CHAD BEGUELIN
Music by MATTHEW SKLAR

WE LOOK TO YOU

Lyrics by CHAD BEGUELIN
Music by MATTHEW SKLAR

Ballad, in 2

peo - ple dance in u - ni - son and no one won - ders why.

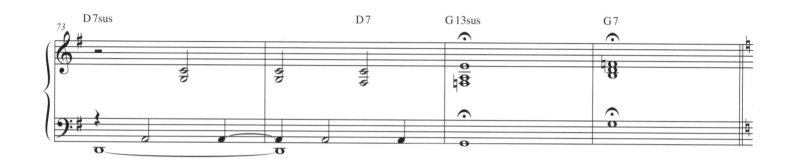

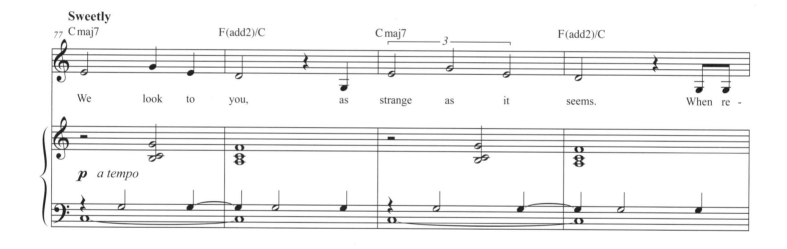

Sweetly

We look to you, as strange as it seems. When re -

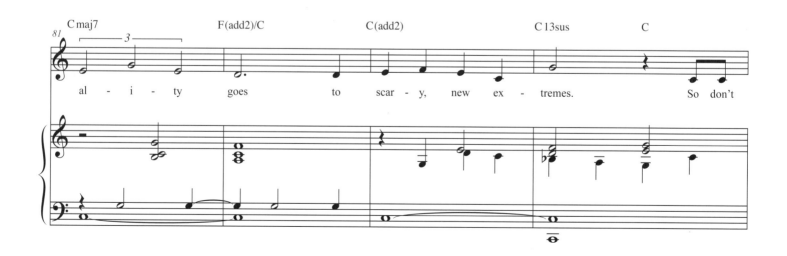

al - i - ty goes to scar - y, new ex - tremes. So don't

TONIGHT BELONGS TO YOU

Lyrics by CHAD BEGUELIN
Music by MATTHEW SKLAR

Bouncy Shuffle, Swing 8ths

I can

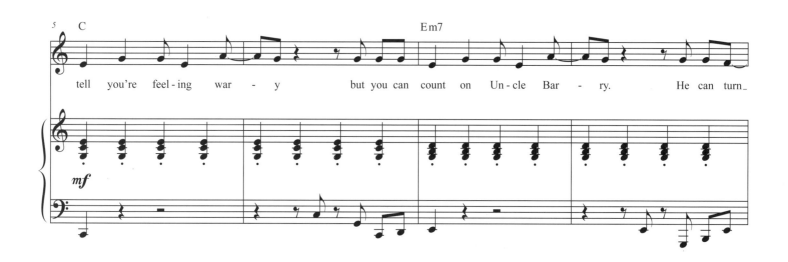

tell you're feel-ing war—y but you can count on Un-cle Bar—ry. He can turn

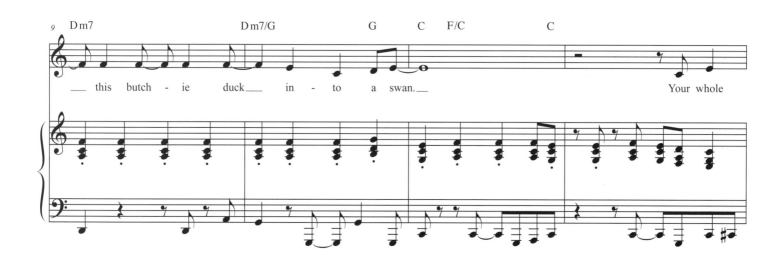

___ this butch—ie duck___ in—to a swan.___ Your whole

ZAZZ

Lyrics by CHAD BEGUELIN
Music by MATTHEW SKLAR

Jazzy 4, Swing 8ths

ANGIE: When a chal-lenge lies a-head and you are filled with dread and wor-ry.

Give it some zazz! If your cour-age dis-ap-pears, what-'ll get your fears to

scur-ry?_____ Give it some zazz! Zazz is style plus con-fi-dence._

THE LADY'S IMPROVING

Lyrics by CHAD BEGUELIN
Music by MATTHEW SKLAR

LOVE THY NEIGHBOR

Lyrics by CHAD BEGUELIN
Music by MATTHEW SKLAR

Bright Gospel feel, in 2

TRENT:
Kay - lee has a small tat - too.

That tat - too would be ta - boo.

Kay - lee, guess what waits for you.

Love____ thy neigh - bor____ trumps them____ all!

Not to o - ver - sim - pli - fy,

but the scrip - ture does im - ply_____

that your mom will have to die._____

How's to - mor - row, if she's not got an - y. plans?

There's no way to sep - a - rate

82

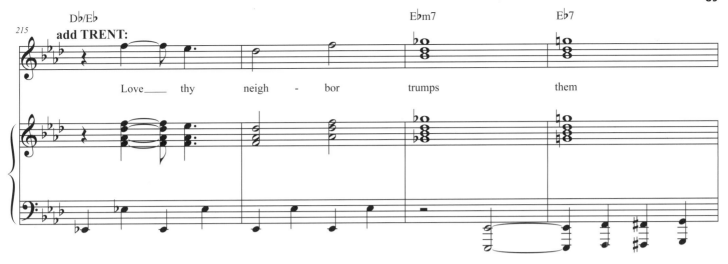

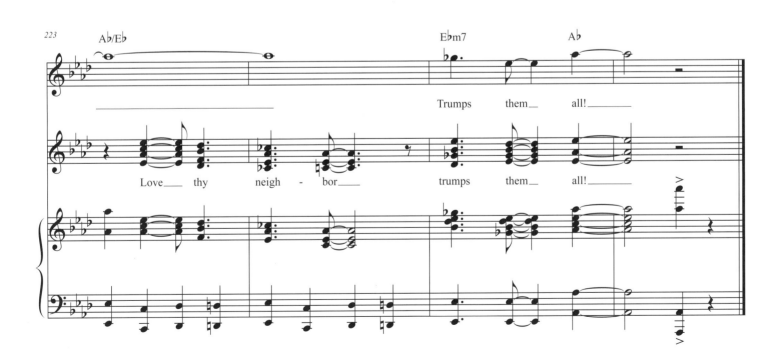

ALYSSA GREENE

Lyrics by CHAD BEGUELIN
Music by MATTHEW SKLAR

Aggressive, angry

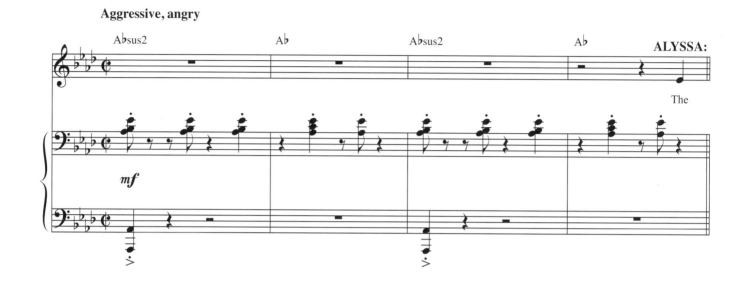

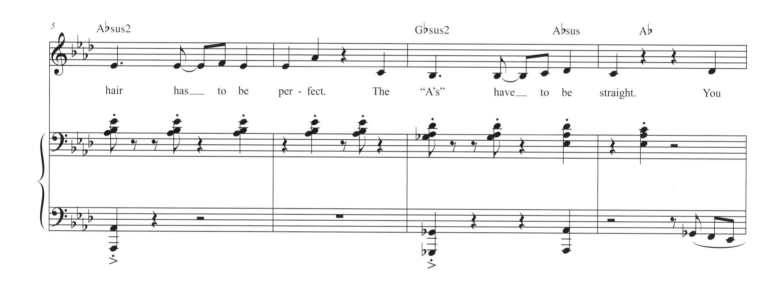

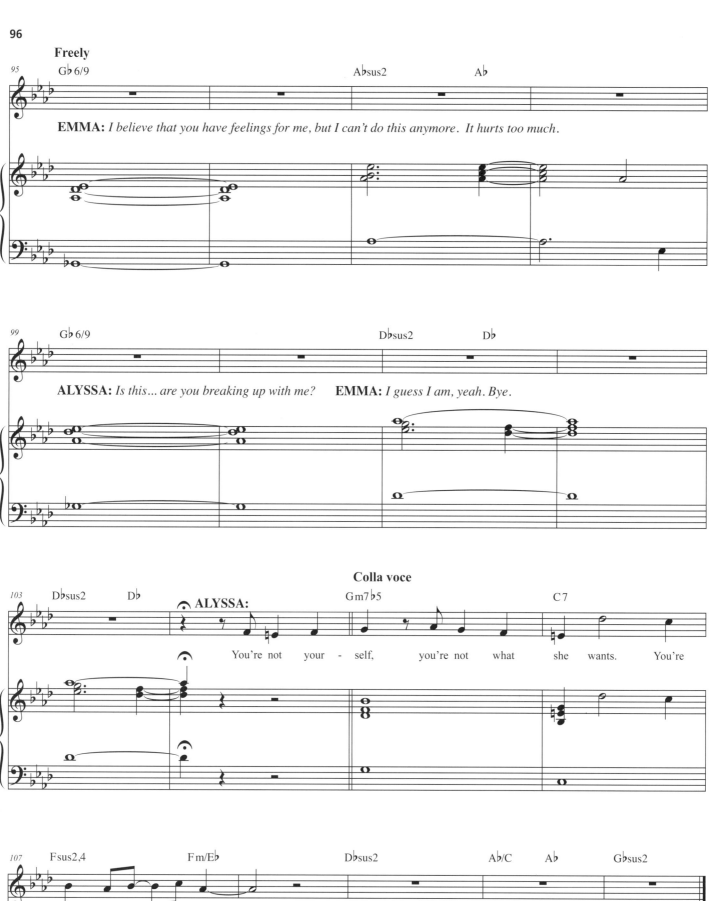

EMMA: *I believe that you have feelings for me, but I can't do this anymore. It hurts too much.*

ALYSSA: *Is this... are you breaking up with me?*   **EMMA:** *I guess I am, yeah. Bye.*

Colla voce

ALYSSA:

You're not your - self, you're not what she wants. You're

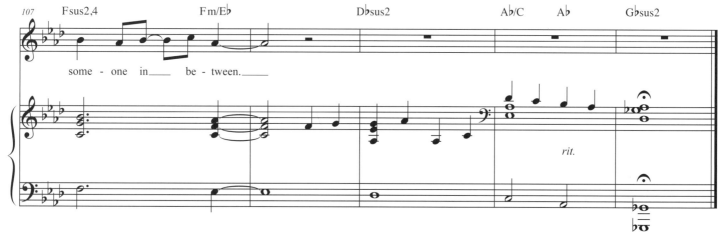

some - one in be - tween.

BARRY IS GOING TO PROM

Lyrics by CHAD BEGUELIN
Music by MATTHEW SKLAR

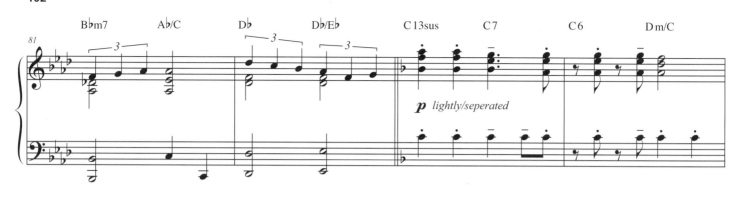

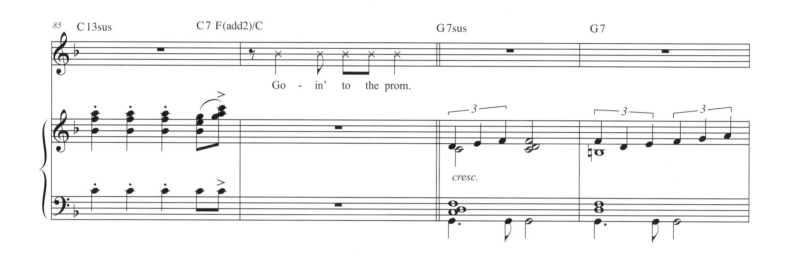

Go - in' to the prom.

In

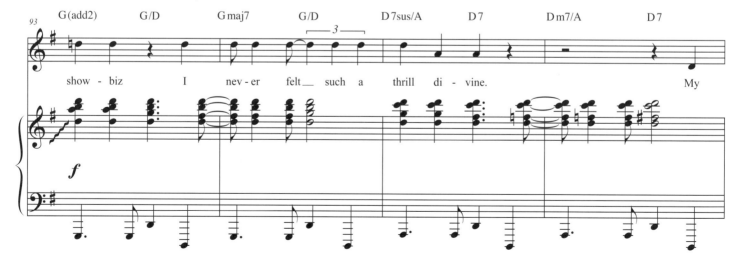

show - biz I nev - er felt___ such a thrill di - vine.

My

UNRULY HEART

Lyrics by CHAD BEGUELIN
Music by MATTHEW SKLAR

Some hearts can con-form, __ fit-ting the norm, __ flaunt-ing their love __ for all __ to see. __

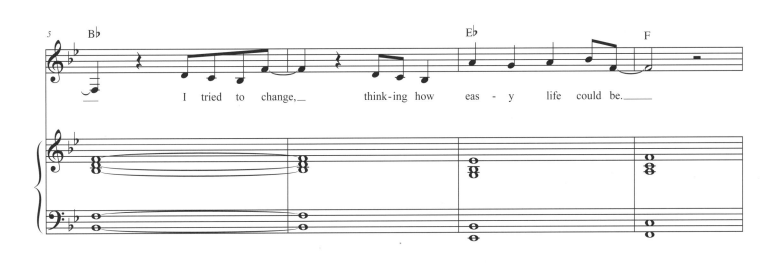

I tried to change, __ think-ing how eas - y life could be. __

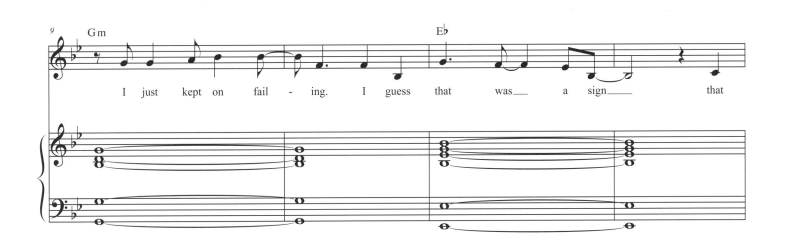

I just kept on fail - ing. I guess that was __ a sign __ that

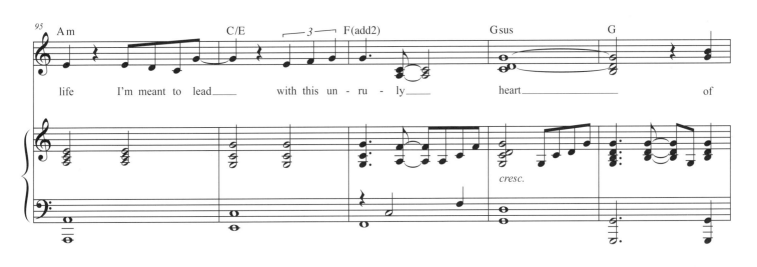

IT'S TIME TO DANCE

Lyrics by CHAD BEGUELIN
Music by MATTHEW SKLAR

Slower

cares what___ oth-er peo-ple say!___ And when we're through,

no one___ can con-vince us we were wrong.___

All it takes___ is you and___ me

Fast 4

EMMA:

and a song.___